ROBERT MAGEE

THE CLASSIC
WORLD OF HORSES

INTRODUCTION BY WILLIAM STEINKRAUS

ARCO

New York

ACKNOWLEDGEMENTS

This book owes its existence to the encouragement and support of two people.

Vello Muikma of Toronto is the professional. Over the years he has given me expert advice, has reproduced my photographs with superb craftsmanship and, most important of all, has believed that my work is worth while.

The amateur is my wife Jane, who has accompanied me for miles under a burden of camera equipment, has taken in stride the domestic chaos I so frequently created, and has acted as a friendly, discriminating and frequently biased critic.

It is a pleasure to express my indebtedness to both of them.

Published by Arco Publishing Company, Inc.
219 Park Avenue South, New York, N.Y. 10003
Copyright © 1974 by Robert Magee
All rights reserved
Library of Congress Catalog Card Number 73-93951
ISBN 0-668-03466-1
Printed in the United States of America

CONTENTS

INTRODUCTION

When Bob Magee introduced himself to me a couple of years ago and modestly inquired if I'd care to glance at some horse pictures he'd taken, I'll have to admit that I didn't expect very much.

Not that I don't enjoy looking at horse pictures — quite the contrary. In fact, one of the first outlets for my passion for horses, starting at about age eight, was clipping magazine pictures of them and pasting them into enormous scrapbooks.

Since then I've missed few chances to study any and every kind of portrayal of the noble animal, from Ming jades to the photo-finish of yesterday's last race, with all stops in between. But frankly, if you like horse pictures well enough to go out of your way to look at them, you get to see an awful lot of mediocre work. For few achievements seem more difficult than the artistic representation of the horse, and this applies equally to every graphic medium.

Part of the difficulty lies in the fact that the horse is a living being of determinate structure and a highly evocative image, and thus means many different things to many different kinds of people. Highly romantic portrayals of horses have always been popular, for example, with maiden aunts and other unhorsey people, though from the horseman's point of view the qualities 'idealized' have often been the wrong ones. (Spirited prancing, though pleasing to the eye, is hard on the seat, and those wonderfully delicate equine limbs simply look weedy to the rider, threatening future unsoundness.) But that which the romantic painter destroys with exaggeration or insufficient knowledge, the literalist (or fast shutter) can kill just as dead, by freezing it into a rigidly static pose that exists in reality only as part of a continuum of movement.

Thus pictures which horsemen admire often leave the layman cold;

though anatomically correct and an accurate record of color and markings, they capture as little of life as the average passport photo and, in that, embody just as great a falsehood. In short, then, horse pictures that are merely competent are scarce enough, whether on canvas or on film, and pictures which also capture something of the essence of an individual or a kind of activity — pictures which convey something of the truth about horses, as Hemingway might put it — are rare indeed.

Feeling this way, I could hardly have been more surprised when Bob produced a collection of some of the most striking color prints I'd ever seen, of horses from all over the world, varied as to breed, type and situation, but all recorded with a most felicitous combination of technical skill and artistic imagination. Many of these pictures appear on the following pages, and the reader will be able to share the pleasant sensation of unanticipated delight that struck me.

Perhaps if I had known that Bob was a top-notch art director for a major advertising agency, who was simply applying a trained eye and a highly professional instinct for design, impact and communication to his avocation, I wouldn't have been quite so surprised. But probably not, for the thing that really sets his work apart is not its technical proficiency per se, but the genuine feeling for horses that motivates it. Bob's pictures are a labor of love, and in the very nicest sense, it shows.

A year or so after my first look at Bob's pictures he showed me the dummy of the present book, and I was happy to be able to play a small role in finding a publisher for it. I can only hope that the wider audience that will now have an opportunity to see what he can do with a camera, and a horse to point it at, will derive as much pleasure from his pictures as I have.

William Steinkraus
Captain of the United States
Equestrian Team from 1955 to 1972
Individual Gold Medalist 1968 Olympic Games

PLEASURE

Since the dawn of history, the association and interdependence of man and his horse have been evident. Records are available from many sources—the writings of the Old Testament, the art of the Greeks, and the monuments and sculptures of the Romans.

Throughout the ages, the horse was the power tool of man. He was used for travel and exploration, for the heavy work of the farm and the transportation of goods, and for speed and mobility in warfare. But he was more than that. He was a friend and companion, a source of pride and admiration, a joyful participant in riding for its own sake and in the games and contests which were an inevitable part of his life with his master.

His pre-eminence in all of these functions was maintained until the twentieth century. It is true that the discovery of gunpowder and the development of improved firepower reduced his importance in warfare, but the decline of the horse as a power instrument awaited the birth of the internal combustion engine. The tractor took over the farm duties, the motor car the transportation, and the tank the warfare.

And yet, although we no longer see the horse drawing carriages and delivery vans on the streets, or hauling plows in the fields, we are amazed to discover that his numbers are increasing and that his quality is being maintained and improved through selective breeding. He still retains his utility on the range, but he is being used more and more simply for the pleasure that he gives mankind.

The
Arabian

It is fitting that the first picture in this book is that of an Arabian, the most distinguished horse in the history of the world and the main source of quality in almost every modern breed.

The Arabian was known as far back as 5000 B.C., and was justly famous in Arabia, Egypt, and Syria. Because of the rigors of the climate and terrain, and through very careful breeding over the centuries, the Arabian developed into the epitome of speed and endurance.

Arabians, which even in ancient times were of tremendous value, were often given as gifts by kings and princes, and thus were introduced into different parts of the world. They accompanied the Moslem conquerors on their excursions across North Africa and into Spain, where they were the foundation stock of the famous Spanish horses from which, among others, the Lipizzaners are descended. Early importations into England included the Byerley Turk in 1689, the Darley Arabian in 1705, and the Godolphin Arabian in 1728; the lineage of virtually every Thoroughbred in the world today can be traced from these famous sires. While the Thoroughbred has replaced the Arabian for racing over the short distances of the modern racetrack, he offers no competition in speed coupled with endurance over long distances.

The Arabian serves man in many ways. He is highly prized for breeding, since almost any kind of horse can be improved by Arabian blood. He is extremely versatile, performing equally well in light harness, jumping in the field, or undertaking the varied duties of a Western stock horse. He is unequalled as a pleasure horse, and is a universal favorite at horse shows where he is often displayed in the native trappings of his original desert home.

Riding

There is a big difference in distance and style between the elegantly dressed horseman riding along a bridle path in Hyde Park, London, and the cowboy rigged riders on the Eaton Ranch near Cody, Wyoming. But the difference is apparent rather than real; the participants share the same goal— the sheer pleasure of riding.

In the United States, the Western movie has played a part in stimulating an interest in life on the range for millions of spectators, and the Dude Ranch has provided thousands of them with an opportunity to participate. Adventurous guests rise at dawn to assist the regular hands in driving a herd of horses from their nighttime range to the corral, while the more timorous sit in the warm early light and dream about the exploits of their heroes, human and equine.

But who can blame all of them for choosing a ride along trails with the blue Wyoming hills in the distance, rather than the traffic and smog of the freeways?

The Hunt

The hunt involves a completely different kind of riding. It demands great speed, endurance, and jumping ability on the part of the horse, and, since it is a group activity, it calls not only for a high degree of skill, courage, and competitive spirit on the part of the rider but also for consideration for the other members of the hunt and the animals involved in the chase.

The stag was hunted in the forests and woodlands of England for centuries. The English horses were slow but good jumpers, and endured the long hours of riding well. As the forests gradually disappeared, the number of stags declined and sportsmen discovered that the fox, until then considered only as vermin fit for quick extinction, was a good substitute.

The first fox hunt organized as a sporting event was held at Belvoir in 1730, and others followed quickly. Somewhat rowdy in character at first, hunts gained in popularity and respectability, and English country life developed around fox hunting. Since the fox ran fast in the open country, there was a need for better horses, and it became the practice to use Thoroughbred sires to breed horses which were superbly suited to the demands of the sport.

Fox hunting is a national institution in England, where conditions are favorable: the winters are mild, the ground is generally smooth, and the English hedge is safer than the wire fence used in many other countries. The sport has become popular in other parts of the world, particularly in Ireland, France, and the United States; with the great increase in wealth and leisure enjoyed by large segments of the population, it seems destined to expand and flourish.

COMPETITION

The origin of the horse show is lost in the past, although it probably owes its start to the early fairs where horses were offered for sale. As early as the fourteenth century, some sportsmen became more interested in the performance of the horses than in the hunt itself, and over the years their impromptu competitions developed into the modern, structured spectacle we enjoy today.

The horse show is truly the showcase of the world of horses; it provides a fascinating blend of rapid pace, superb horsemanship, and incomparable splendor. Horse shows come in all shapes and sizes, from the country fair and the small-town agricultural exhibition to the elaborate, highly organized, many event show of the large metropolitan center. They include competitions as traditional as the Harness classes of proud Hackneys and Shetlands, as tense and exhilarating as the Jumpers contending with a planned series of obstacles, or as beautiful as the Saddle Horses whose unique characteristic is the ability to execute five gaits, a talent possessed by no other breed in the world.

The horse show is also a proving ground where the effect of sound breeding is measured. The performing ability as well as the general appearance and bearing of one horse can be compared with that of another, and the champions of the show ring have a lot to do with improving the quality of the lesser horses which serve for pleasure and utility.

The spectacular and often hazardous jumping of horses, whether in open country following the hounds, racing in the steeplechase, or in the horse show with its carefully arranged pattern of varied obstacles, is a thrilling sight even to those who are not particularly familiar with equestrian events.

For many centuries it was not necessary for horses to jump, either in battle or sport, except for an occasional ditch or small bank. After the passage of the Enclosure Act in eighteenth-century England it was no longer possible to gallop across country without jumping fences, and riders quickly became aware of the fact that the horse is a natural jumper and began to experience the thrill of this new form of horsemanship.

Jumping was slow to gain recognition, however, and the first recorded competition was at a harness show in Paris in 1866. The competitors appeared in the ring to parade before the spectators and then went into the adjoining countryside to jump over natural obstacles. Since it was difficult to attract interest under these conditions, the next development was the erection of a few fences in the horse show arena itself. Show jumping had to wait to gain recognition as a major event; equestrian competitions were not included in the Olympic Games until 1912.

There are two general categories of performers: the hunter and the jumper. The hunter is usually a Thoroughbred ridden in the field with hounds; his conformation, way of moving, and performance are all considered in judging him. The jumper can be of any breed and is scored entirely on his performance; he must have spirit, intelligence, and great size and strength.

In a jumping competition penalties are incurred by faults such as knocking down an obstacle, refusing to jump, or the fall of the horse or rider. In some cases, particularly when the contest has ended in a tie, the time taken to complete the course is a determining factor.

International Show Jumping

International show jumping is judged in accordance with the rules and regulations of the Federation Equestre International. The course is carefully planned; it varies in length from six hundred to a thousand yards, and the turns demand changes in direction. Some obstacles require the horse to spread himself, as in the case of water, while others test the horse's ability to jump a great height, as in the case of a wall or gate. Fences are usually between four feet three inches and five feet high, and are solid in appearance. International show jumping is a test not only of the jumping capability of the horse, but also of his obedience and speed.

The Olympic Show Jumping Grand Prix is the most important jumping competition, a magnificent spectacle in which the efficiency and quality of horses and riders from numerous countries are tested and compared.

The national teams consist of four horses and four riders. Each horse and rider completes the course twice, with a short interval between turns. There are twenty obstacles of every conceivable difficulty, and the flowing continuity of spectacular jumps has made the Grand Prix one of the most distinguished of all Olympic events. It is for this reason that it has been chosen as the closing ceremony of the Olympic Games.

Dressage

Dressage, in its simplest as well as most advanced form, signifies the fine training of a horse. Its purpose is to perfect all of his natural movements and to make him keen, obedient, supple, well-balanced, and completely responsive to the direction of his rider, even when unnoticeable by the spectator.

Training begins at an elementary level and advances to the high standard of the Grand Prix. The Grand Prix dressage competition is designed to show the horse's qualities and training in all of the elementary school gaits plus the fundamental gaits of the Haute École. The program consists of thirty-three exercises performed in twelve and a half minutes, done from memory and in strict routine, and judged by an international jury appointed by the International Equestrian Federation. The champions are those horses which display, to the greatest extent, beauty, gentleness, intelligence, and sensitivity to the lightest command of the rider.

The Three-Day Event

The three-day event was introduced over seventy years ago as a test for cavalry horses to ensure that no phase of their training had been neglected. Appropriately enough, the competition was called "The Military," and it has been changed little since its inception. It is often called the "complete test" of horse and rider, and it is the most exciting and exhausting of the international equestrian competitions.

The same team of horse and rider competes in three separate events on three consecutive days. The first day consists of an intermediate type of dressage, less complicated than the Grand Prix but still designed to demonstrate fully the horse's willingness, training, and obedience.

The second day is the endurance test covering twenty-five miles and combining roads and trails, a steeplechase, and a cross-country course. It is ridden over a varied terrain with some thirty-five obstacles of all kinds, and includes an all-out sprint to the finish line. Most of the spills occur in this event, and rarely do more than half of the contestants finish the race.

Despite the exhaustion of the horses and riders, on the third day they are required (after a veterinary examination) to enter a stadium jumping test which, although less formidable than the Grand Prix, makes still further demands on the skill, courage, and endurance of the participants.

The final standings are determined by totaling the penalties, less any bonus points, of the best three out of the four horses and riders from each competing nation. The horse and rider with the lowest penalty score wins the individual championship.

It is little wonder that the winner of the Olympic gold medal is regarded as the world's equestrian champion—and this is true both of the rider and of the horse which made his championship possible.

Polo   Polo, which originated in Persia about 600 B.C., is one of the oldest recorded games in the world. Over the centuries it spread to all parts of Asia, including China, Japan, and India. British soldiers learned the game in India and brought it back to England about the middle of the nineteenth century, and it spread to continental Europe and America at a somewhat later date.

Two teams of four players each compete on the large field. A full game consists of eight periods, called chukkers, seven and a half minutes long, with intervals of three minutes between chukkers. The players ride horses which are referred to as ponies, and their objective is to use their long-handled mallets to drive a wooden ball through the opposing goalposts, eight feet wide, at the ends of the field. One point is scored each time the ball goes through the goalposts.

This is a hard game, often involving bodily contact between horses and riders, and calls for great endurance and agility as well as for coordination between the rider and his mount. The well-trained polo pony reacts almost automatically to the lightning pace of top competition: he will stop on a dime, spin in his tracks, and take off at top speed in the opposite direction at any moment during the contest. The fact that he plays for no more than two chukkers in a game, with a rest of at least one chukker in between, is an indication of the great demands the game makes on his strength and spirit.

The Rodeo

The rodeo is a major sports spectacular in the United States and Canada today and annually attracts millions of spectators and offers millions of dollars in prize money to the winners. It developed from the everyday work on the cattle range.

It was inevitable that the cowboys would challenge each other in contests such as bronco busting, steer wrestling, calf roping, and bull riding. It was equally inevitable that these contests would be organized for public viewing. The first recorded event of this kind was held at Cheyenne, Wyoming, a hundred years ago. Later developments included giving prize money to the winners of the different events and charging admission, and this marked the beginning of the rodeo as a large commercial enterprise.

The popularity of the rodeo is easy to understand. The many different events are rough and dangerous, demanding strength, skill, and courage. They pit man against animal in a panorama of color and excitement mixed with flashes of humor and, more often than not, the achievement of the apparently impossible.

Despite the tumult, each event has its own rules. In saddle bronc riding the rider must come out of the chute spurring, and continue to spur from shoulder to flank throughout the ten-second ride, keeping one hand in the air; if he touches any part of the horse or saddle with either hand he is marked down for "pulling leather." The contestant is scored both on his ride and on how hard the horse bucks.

Bareback riding is strictly a one-hand contest lasting eight seconds; to qualify, the rider's spurs must be over the break of the bronc's shoulders during the first jump out. Pickup men in the arena release the flank strap and lift the contestant off when the time has expired.

The calf-roping event pits a cowboy on a highly disciplined Quarter Horse in a race against time. Teamwork, skill, timing, maneuverability, and speed go into this performance by horse and rider where split seconds count. The calf is given a thirty-foot start; a good horse follows him, keeps him in proper position, and stops immediately when the loop is thrown. Then the horse must keep the right tension on the rope while the rider throws the calf and makes the tie.

The racing events include the chuck wagon race, where teams of four compete furiously to load camping gear into the rear of the wagons, form a figure eight around two barrels, and then move onto the track for the sprint to the finish line. In the wild horse race, each team of three contestants tries to saddle one of sixteen horses and ride it across the finish line within the prescribed time limit.

For any horse lover craving wild action, the rodeo is certainly too good to miss!

PERFORMANCE

To people in many lands, the scarlet tunics of the Royal Canadian Mounted Police, mounted on their black horses, are as well known as the Maple Leaf on the Canadian flag.

Organized shortly after Canadian Confederation in 1873, the "Mounties" played an important part in the peaceful settlement and development of the Western Provinces by establishing the rule of law prior to the mass influx of homesteaders. Today they are recognized as one of the world's great national police forces.

The famous Musical Ride was first performed in 1876, only three years after the founding of the Force, and since that time has been seen by millions of spectators at events as different as the Coronation of Queen Elizabeth, the Canadian National Exhibition, and Expo 1970, in Tokyo.

The Musical Ride, a variety of intricate movements performed to musical selections at different tempos, is presented by a full troop of thirty-two men and horses. Developed through the years as cavalry exercises, these figures enable the rider to gain the confidence and complete control of his mount. They demand the utmost in coordination and timing since the figures are performed by individuals, twos, fours, and eights at the trot and the canter.

The climax is described in a Royal Canadian Mounted Police program:

"Perhaps the highlight of each performance is the Charge. The horses stamp and fret impatiently as they await the chilling trumpet notes . . . crimson-tipped lances of the foremost ranks arc down to the Engage . . . and eager mounts and ready riders catapult forward at the Gallop."

Every small boy waits with bated breath to hear his father say the magic words, "Let's go to the circus." Little does he know, or care, that the Greeks taught horses to dance and bow as early as 500 B.C., that the Romans engaged in chariot racing and trick riding, or that performing horses and dancing bears amused the crowds at medieval fairs. He is quite content to sit spellbound and watch the clowns, the trapeze artists, the wild animals, and especially the horses.

The modern circus dates from the middle of the eighteenth century, when jugglers and acrobats first used bareback mounts. It was at about this time that Philip Astley, a former British cavalry sergeant-major who was making his living teaching acrobatics and horsemanship, discovered that it was easy to maintain balance while standing on a horse cantering in a circle, and soon all the performances were conducted in an enclosed ring, forty-two feet in diameter, and with a covered stand. The Astley and Franconi circuses in England and France became as famous as their American counterparts, Barnum and Bailey and the Ringling Brothers.

Three types of horses perform in the circus, and all are given highly specialized training. Liberty horses, which perform without riders, are usually Arabs or have Arabian blood, and are carefully selected to match in size and color. High School horses are given training similar to that used in preparing for dressage contests, but more spectacular movements must be learned to appeal to the circus audiences. Rosinbacks, named from the practice of rubbing rosin on their backs to prevent the performer from slipping, are the bareback riding horses on which one or several artists vault, jump, build pyramids, and do other hair-raising feats.

The horse is truly the king of circus life, and the bareback riders are the elite of circus society.

The Spanish Riding School

Many visitors to Vienna avail themselves of the opportunity to visit the Spanish Riding School, the home of the famous Lipizzaner stallions and the last riding academy in the world where classical horsemanship is still cultivated in its purest form.

Spanish horses containing Arab blood were first bred in Austria about 1562 on the initiative of the Archduke who was to become Emperor Maximilian II. A few years later a royal stud was established at Lipizza, where specially selected animals were raised under the favorable conditions of the area, and breeding was carefully controlled. Although the Spanish Riding School dates back to this period, the beautiful building in which the Lipizzaners perform is of later origin and was completed in 1735.

The story of the magnificent achievements of the Spanish Riding School, as well as its trials and tribulations through wars, revolutions, and even earthquakes, reads like fiction. Its dangers and dislocations during the Napoleonic struggle are matched only by the heroic efforts of the head of the school, Colonel Alois Podhajsky (with the assistance of General Patton and the United States Army) to save the horses during World War II. Today the Spanish Riding School is one of Austria's greatest national treasures.

A performance of the Spanish Riding School is a demonstration of the whole education of the Lipizzaners. It begins with a display of the young stallions which come from the stud farm at the age of four. It continues with the fully trained stallions performing all of the difficult exercises and paces of the Haute École to the sound of music. These include the pirouette, the flying charge, piaffe, and passage, and all the exercises demanded for the Olympic dressage tests.

The performance moves towards its climax with the preparation for the exercises above the ground. Some exercises are copied from nature, like the play and fighting of horses in the pasture; others are adaptations of maneuvers formerly used in combat. In the "Airs Above the Ground" the stallions and riders, who perform without stirrups, stand motionless in the levade and jump high into the air in caprioles, courbettes, and ballotades. The finale is the traditional Great School Quadrille, a series of intricate steps brilliantly performed in unison by eight or twelve riders.

The Spanish Riding School remains faithful to its traditions; its performance, whether at home in Vienna or on its occasional world tours, continues to serve as an example of the harmony between horse and rider which is emblematic of the classical art of riding.

RACING

Racing has often been called the Sport of Kings, and it is true that many kings have indulged in it. But it is also the sport of the common man who, as a spectator, attends race meetings by the millions.

Historically it was inevitable that whenever men and horses came together wagers would be made and races run. Even in ancient times horse races were major events; Plutarch indicated their relative importance with the remarkable observation that "Philip the father of Alexander the Great received three glad tidings in a single day: that the Illyrians were conquered by Parmenio, that his horse had won at Olympia, and that a son was born unto him."

In seventeenth-century England, racing usually involved two country gentlemen betting on the quality of their horses and going to the nearby heath to vindicate their bets. If the neighbors turned up and joined the race, the winner had to eliminate them all. The Stuart kings loved hunting and racing, and each year they moved their Court to the favorable countryside at Newmarket. By the end of the century regular meetings were held and, although many of the gentry continued to ride their own horses, professionals were often used. With the growth of betting and the increase in the number of races, it became increasingly necessary to establish a body which could enforce rules of conduct, and the Jockey Club was founded about 1750. Rules were laid down, meetings were properly organized, entries were controlled, and race horses were bred scientifically.

All Thoroughbreds trace their ancestry to three Arabian stallions imported into England: the Darley Arabian, the Byerley Turk, and the Godolphin Arabian; and through their respective descendants: Eclipse, Herod, and Matchem. On the female side, Thoroughbred quality is derived from not more than about forty original foundation mares, a number of which were Arabians imported by Charles II. Breeding records were originally kept only by individual owners, but recordkeeping was improved by the publication of the first Racing Calendar in 1727, and by the introduction of the General Stud Book with its great wealth of breeding information some sixty years later. A hundred years ago there were only a few thousand Thoroughbreds, chiefly those registered in the English General Stud Book; today they are numbered in the hundreds of thousands in all parts of the world.

While Thoroughbreds are used in jumping races—hurdle races over relatively low hurdles or steeplechases over higher shrubbery fences—most people associate them with flat racing in contests which may be only locally recognized or which may be as famous as the Canadian Queen's Plate, the oldest race run continuously in North America and already in its fifteenth year when the Kentucky Derby was run for the first time; or as famous as the "Triple Crowns"—the Kentucky Derby (1874), Preakness (1873), and Belmont Stakes (1863) in the United States; and the 2000 Guineas (1809), Epsom Derby (1780), and St. Leger (1778) in England.

Winning a Triple Crown is one of the rarest achievements in the whole field of sporting events, and the odds against it grow longer every year.

The English Triple Crown was won by the Aga Khan's Bahram in 1935, but thirty-five years elapsed before the great champion Nijinsky duplicated this feat in 1970. In the United States it took a quarter of a century (1948–1973) before Secretariat duplicated Citation's winning of the Triple Crown. In Citation's day there were only about 6000 three-year-olds on the register of the Jockey Club; but Secretariat had 25,000 potential competitors in his age group.

The Standardbred

Harness racing enjoys wide popularity, particularly in America, where the Standardbred was developed through careful breeding in order to create a racehorse which combined the ability to pace or trot at high speed with the endurance required to run heat after heat without flagging. This goal was achieved by establishing a "Standard" in 1880, and barring all animals which could not meet the stated qualifications. The Standard has been revised periodically, so that today this famous American breed, like that of the Thoroughbred, has become a "closed corporation."

The Steeplechase

The steeplechase developed from the pounding matches to which Irish gentry challenged each other—gruelling cross-country races in which everyone followed the leader and the last survivor was named the winner. A limit was eventually put on the distance by racing to a conspicuous landmark such as a church steeple.

Today the two greatest events of this kind are the Grand National and the Maryland Hunt Club Steeplechase. The Grand National, held at Aintree, England, is run twice around a beautiful flat turf course, and covers a total distance of four and a half miles with over thirty brush fences all about five feet in height. There are many starters, both professional and amateur, and the frequent spills add to the excitement and the hazards of the race.

The Maryland Hunt Club Steeplechase, held at Glyndon, Maryland, is a four-mile course over extremely difficult country with twenty-two solidly fixed timber fences. Unlike the Grand National, it is a single event, and no professional may ride in it. There is no grandstand, no admission fee, and no fixed starting gate. It is probably the most famous race in the world which still bears the hallmarks of a strictly amateur event.

CONCLUSION

It is reassuring to know that the horse, although supplanted from many of his former tasks by the development of the machine, is in no danger of extinction. He is a companion and friend in the search for some hours of leisure enjoyment, and perhaps even a way of life free from the social and psychological hazards imposed on us by our crowded, hustled, frenzied day-by-day existence.

The author hopes that the following pictures will help you to capture the spirit of this noble animal and to appreciate his association with mankind today and in the days ahead.

PLEASURE

COMPETITION

43

44

47

66

68

94

95

PERFORMANCE

RACING

DOUBLE CHOICE PRICES
COMBINING NUMBER WITH
EXACTOR
3AND6
PAYS 54.30
CORRECTIONS
TELETIME
FINISH 157
1303
1002
291

124

NOTES ON THE PLATES (BY PAGE NUMBER)